County Durham & Yorkshire
Edited by Donna Samworth

First published in Great Britain in 2016 by:

Remus House
Coltsfoot Drive
Peterborough
PE2 9BF
Telephone: 01733 890066
Website: www.youngwriters.co.uk
All Rights Reserved
Book Design by Ashley Janson
© Copyright Contributors 2015
SB ISBN 978-1-78624-070-5

Printed and bound in the UK by BookPrintingUK
Website: www.bookprintinguk.com

Foreword

Welcome, Reader!

For Young Writers' latest competition, *Poetry Emotions*, we gave school children nationwide the task of writing a poem all about emotions, and they rose to the challenge magnificently!

Pupils could either write about emotions they've felt themselves or create a character to represent an emotion. Which one they chose was entirely up them. Our aspiring poets have also developed their creative skills along the way, getting to grips with poetic techniques such as rhyme, simile and alliteration to bring their thoughts to life. The result is this entertaining collection that allows us a fascinating glimpse into the minds of the next generation, giving us an insight into their innermost feelings. It also makes a great keepsake for years to come.

Here at Young Writers our aim is to encourage creativity in children and to inspire a love of the written word, so it's great to get such an amazing response, with some absolutely fantastic poems. This made it a tough challenge to pick the winners, so well done to *Libbie Frostick* who has been chosen as the best author in this anthology.

I'd like to congratulate all the young authors in *Poetry Emotions - County Durham & Yorkshire* - I hope this inspires them to continue with their creative writing.

Jenni Bannister
Editorial Manager

Our charity partner for this academic year is ...

YOUNGMINDS

The voice for young people's **mental health and wellbeing**

We're aiming to raise a huge £5,000 this academic year to help raise awareness for YoungMinds and the great work they do to support children and young people.

If you would like to get involved visit
www.justgiving.com/Young-Writers

YoungMinds is the UK's leading charity committed to improving the emotional wellbeing and mental health of children and young people. They campaign, research and influence policy and practice on behalf of children and young people to improve care and services. They also provide expert knowledge to professionals, parents and young people through the Parents' Helpline, online resources, training and development, outreach work and publications. Their mission is to improve the emotional resilience of all children and to ensure that those who suffer ill mental health get fast and effective support.

www.youngminds.org.uk

Contents

George Wilson Close 1

Crystal Gardens Primary School, Bradford
Khadija Mrihel 1

Kirby Hill CE Primary School, York
Harry Sellers (9) 2
Harry Burland (9) 2
Clark Gibson (8) 3
William Lenton (9) 3
Jessica Green (9) 3
Sophie Robson (9) 4
Kieran Tyler Hale (8) 4
Lauren Welford (9) 4
Thomas Morgan Salvini (8) 5
Aaron Alastair Chandler (9) 5

Oxbridge Lane Primary School, Stockton-on-Tees
Alisha Hussain 5
Husna Qayyum (9) 6
Hafeez Farooq 6
Mia Hall 7
Rosie Partridge (9) 7
Ndumiso Ndlovu 8
Aiden Binks 8
Isa Salim 9
Natasha Rogers 9
Emily Dishi (9) 10
Safaa Khaliq 10
Grace Gibson 11
Leonardo Dogjani (9) 11
Shamaar McBlain 12
Aman Habib 12
Mille-Ann Hutchinson 13
Melisa Kirschmann (9) 13
Nicole Nyilika (9) 14
Harris Ali 14
Demi-Kaia Patridge 15
Adam Ali 15
Rheis Stephenson 16

Caleigh Savage 16
Mayson Swainston 17
Shiza Ahmed (9) 17
Sana Ibrar Hussain (9) 18
Brandon-Kai Dent 18
Thomas Bacon 19
Mia Durham 19
Aribah Naveed 20
Markus Lawson (9) 20
Charlie Shepherd 21
Hannah Templeman (9) 21
Calvin Thomas (9) 22
Lexi Bradshaw (9) 22
Brandon Cooper-Lambert (9) 23
Katie Payne 23
Jacob Richardson 24
Jannath Shahzad 24
Scarlett Gardner 25
Alyssa Moody 25
Zain Hussain 26
Millie Lister 26
Alisa Taylor-Hussain 27
Ifrah Sabaat Naveed (8) 27
Jake Sharp 28
Matthew Gittins 28
Mason Beck 29
Bailey Plews 29

Reevy Hill Primary School, Bradford
Danny Ryan (10) 30
Shenai Harney (9) 30
Leon Cunningham (9) 31
Denis Zvonovs (10) 31
Kyle Bower (9) 32
Jaml Leigh Barwell (9) 32
Gavinder Bassra (9) 33
Courtney Mclean (9) 33
Harrison Lee Windsor (9) 34
Phoebe Powell (9) 34
Codie Regan (9) 35
Sarah 35
Lawson Hammond 36

Ebony Cleworth (9) 36

Riverside School, Goole

Sam Stewart (10) 37
Kofi Fricker (10) 38
Luke Dowse (10) 38
Ehsan Mann (10) 39
Beth Sims (10) 39
Oliver Goulsbra Miller (10) 40
Connor Parkinson (10) 40
Jack Gardner (9) 40
Reece Dunn (9) 41
Reece McCrory (9) 41
Mia Cunningham (10) 41

Throston Primary School, Hartlepool

Georgia Thompson (10) 42
Ryan McAllister 43
Maddie Trueman-Wray (9) 44
Tegan Tunstall (9) 45
Ethan Kinnersley (7) 46
Jay Nicholson (9) 46
Emily-Kate Brown (10) 47
Sam Codner (10) 47
Ellie May Ashley (10) 48
Ben Mills (10) 48
Tabitha McQuilling (9) 49
Eve Black (8) 49
Vinny Rowbotham (9) 50
Beth Williamson (10) 50
Will Tighe (9) 51
Ellie Jade Kelsey (10) 51
Faith Evans (9) 52
Kai Arnold (9) 52
Charlotte Scott (10) 53
Lucy White (10) 53
Daniel Hill (10) 54
Alex Trotter (9) 54
Lucie Griffith (9) 55
Jacob George Carney (9) 55
Louie Brown (10) 56
Harry Huntley (9) 56
Katie Pattison (10) 57
Daniel Arnell (10) 57
Ben Green (9) 58
Aidan Howe (8) 58
Naomi Park-Hanson (10) 59

Mollie Jenkins (10) 59
Lara Ann Stewart (7) 60
Trinity Bowman (10) 60
Isabel Hodgson (10) 61
Amy Burton (11) 61
Laura Jukes-Bell (9) 62
Travis Gorton (9) 62
Libbie Frostick (10) 63
Sammy Dhaliwal (9) 63
Lucy Burton (8) 64
Lucy Jasmine Agar (8) 64
Patrick Bainbridge (8) 65
Jonathan Stamper (8) 65
Alyssa Suggitt (10) 66
Summer Elizabeth Inglesant (9) 66
Ben Eglintine (9) 67
Molly McPartlin (10) 67
Maddie Smith 68
Sophie Pattison (8) 68
Tegan Smith (9) 69
Lucy Thompson (7) 69
Keira Vaughan (8) 70
Amber Arnell (7) 70
Luke Steven Swales (10) 71
Rhys Denton (8) 71
Amber Gavillet (10) 72
Joshua Flint (7) 72
Grace Butt (7) 73
Leo Rooke (7) 73
Sam Mills (7) 74
Milly Smith (8) 74
Zachary Unthank (9) 75
Alfie Hastings (8) 75
Jacob Lamb (9) 76
Lilly King (7) 76
Ashley Grant (8) 77
Isabelle Elizabeth Barron (7) 77
Benjamin Barker (10) 78
Alfie Johnson (9) 78
Alivia Crinnion (10) 79
Sonnie Crosman (8) 79
Elise-Jo Stallard (8) 80
Izabel Madison Balch (7) 80
Billy Littlewood (8) 81
Martha Kidd (8) 81
Macey Fleetham-Reid (9) 82
Rebecca Lynn (8) 82

Richard Andrew Barker (8) 83
Viktoria Cooke (7) 83
Lizzy Wilson (7) 84
Emily Alton (8) 84
Jakelynd Khan (9) 85
Nathan Jensen (7) 85
Taylor Crompton (7) 86
Courtney Kennedy (10) 86
Daniel Foster (9) 87
Carson Ibbotson (10) 87
Owen Robson (8) 88
Jacob Luke Robinson (9) 88
Tionne Jane Wyness (9) 88
Ben Alderson (10) 89
Tahlia Smith (7) 89
Kai Hart (10) 89
Benjy Millward (10) 90
Millie Brown (7) 90
Erin Elizabeth Frankland (10) 90
Ryan Kelsey (8) 91
Stanley Ridgway (9) 91
Caleb Christal (9) 91
Alisha Osborne (8) 92
Ben Goodwin (9) 92
Louis Weatherill-Smith (8) 92
Jessica Swinburne 93
Ryan Picknett (10) 93
Kate Muir (10) 93
Sam Littlewood (7) 94

Whale Hill Primary School, Middlesbrough

Jasmine Leigh Pallent (9) 94
Owen Harrison (10) 95
Lillie-Mae Kelly (10) 95
Faith Savage (10) 96
Grace Robinson (10) 96
Katie Marie Power (10) 97
Elle Stainthorpe (10) 97
Alix Huskison (10) 98
Lilymae Hayes (10) 98
Halle Cole (10) 99
Ellie Halliday (10) 99
Hannah Portas (9) 100
Abbie Gibson (10) 100
Jack John Roberts (10) 101
Riley Graeme Kast (10) 101

Jack Edwards (9) 102
Evie Hopper (10) 102
Harley Cruickshank (10) 103
Eleasha Nicole Love (9) 103
Ryan Biggs (9) 104
Jacob Stockton (9) 104
Milly Reed (10) 105
Macie Hellon (9) 105
Cerys James (10) 106
Jessica Adamson (9) 106
Helena Dixon (9) 107
Owen Harding (10) 107
Lewis Clark (9) 108
Sofia Bentley (9) 108
Sean Mullarkey (9) 109
Preston Hayes (9) 109
Sophie-Leigh Wanless (10) 110
Leyla Rukiye Duran (10) 110
Adam Lincoln (9) 111
Madalyn Ruby Horton (9) 111
Alisha Massey (9) 112
Danielle McKittrick (9) 112
Jasmine Colpitts (10) 113
Larry Parsons (9) 113

The Poems

Anger!

If Anger was an animal it would be . . .
A roaring lion stalking his tea,
A big, brave, bold stallion trying to swat a flea,
A giant elephant bumping into a tough tree,
A killer whale on a desert land,
A little grey mouse trapped in a rubber band,
A money spider swallowed by a hand,
And a cranky old camel in Greenland!

George Wilson Close

My Best Birthday Ever

When my birthday came
I had a smile on my face
Soon I played with the water gun
Oops! I shot my aunt's foot
Then I opened my present which was a new TV
We had to go shopping
So I was hopping
We bought a lot of things
which made me think
What a lovely day this is.

Khadija Mrihel
Crystal Gardens Primary School, Bradford

What Am I ?

I go pale and white and suddenly everything goes dark
Ice reminds me of an ice-cold drink
The taste is sour lemon and lime
The sourness makes me shiver
You look down and your knees are like jelly and your teeth are chattering
Ghosts haunting you in a haunted house
Like Antarctica . . . a freezing cold place.

What emotion am I?
Nerves.

Harry Sellers (9)
Kirby Hill CE Primary School, York

Surprised

Surprised is a dark yellow saffron
You go a funny colour when you are surprised
When you are surprised you go a funny purple!
Surprised tastes like dark chocolate melting on my tongue
It is a surprising taste
It smells like a surprising dark chocolate
It is very surprising!
Surprising looks like a famous person has just walked through the door!

Harry Burland (9)
Kirby Hill CE Primary School, York

Surprised

The colour of surprise is the colour of an orange
The colour of an orange is the colour amber
It tastes like a milkshake with melted marshmallows
It smells like a flower from a lavender tree
It looks like a firework exploding into popcorn
It sounds like a squeak of a rabbit
It feels like a stroke of a budgie's feathers.

Clark Gibson (8)
Kirby Hill CE Primary School, York

Anger

Ruby is the colour you feel in anger
It tastes like chilli as your face reddens with anger

It smells like an open wound as you fill with anger
It looks like a creeping spider as your face turns with anger

It sounds like a burning fire as you can't contain your anger
It feels like a demon in your head talking with anger

William Lenton (9)
Kirby Hill CE Primary School, York

Anger

Anger is a ruby-red fire
Anger is expired food stinging your tongue
Anger is smoke puffing in your face
Anger looks like a fire right in front of your face
Anger sounds like screaming and shouting in the house
Anger feels like you could break a wall down with one punch.

Jessica Green (9)
Kirby Hill CE Primary School, York

Surprised

I think of the colour yellow because it is bright
The taste is delicious
The smell makes me hungry
It looks delicious and I want to eat it straight away
It sounds like fireworks
It feels smooth and sticky.

Sophie Robson (9)
Kirby Hill CE Primary School, York

Surprised!

Surprised is a really bright gold,
It tastes like chocolate caramel melting in my mouth,
It smells like daisies.
It looks mouth-popping,
It sounds like a person clapping behind your back,
It feels extraordinary!

Kieran Tyler Hale (8)
Kirby Hill CE Primary School, York

Happy

Happy is a light green
It tastes like chocolate melting on the tip of my tongue
It smells like freshly baked chocolate chip cookies
It looks like a day at the seaside with the sun shining
It sounds like fireworks going off in my head
It feels like my head is about to explode.

Lauren Welford (9)
Kirby Hill CE Primary School, York

Surprise

Surprise is a big bright silver
It tastes like toffee
It smells like daisies
It looks mouth shocking
Someone clapping behind your back
It feels extraordinary.

Thomas Morgan Salvini (8)
Kirby Hill CE Primary School, York

The Anger Poem

The colour of anger is red
Red is an angry colour
The taste of anger is mustard
Mustard is yellow and it is very hot as well
The smell is horrible, it's like mouldy sandwiches and it's horrible.

Aaron Alastair Chandler (9)
Kirby Hill CE Primary School, York

Emotion Poem

I am proud at Fun City,
I slid down the slide but it wasn't pretty.

I get angry when people scare me,
It's not fair, I wish they'd leave me.

I was happy because it was my cousin's birthday
I got her an Elsa present and a card on Thursday.

Alisha Hussain
Oxbridge Lane Primary School, Stockton-on-Tees

Emotion Poem

I felt excited on my birthday when I got lots of things
I got lots of presents including rings
We played lots of games,
And said silly names,
And went round wearing fairy wings.

I was upset when my grandad died
At the age of one hundred and five,
I went downstairs crying
To tell my mam.
My mam told me something but she was lying
But I knew he had died.

Husna Qayyum (9)
Oxbridge Lane Primary School, Stockton-on-Tees

Emotion Poem

I felt excited when I got a bike,
It has lots of spikes,
It was the best
I went on a hike,
And saw a nest,
then had a rest
So my dad got me Nike
That's what I like.

I feel angry when people steal my things,
Sometimes toy cars and sometimes rings,
My sister thinks she can rule
She is always cruel
That's why she steals everything.

Hafeez Farooq
Oxbridge Lane Primary School, Stockton-on-Tees

Emotions Poem

I felt excited when it was Christmas morning,
I was very tired and loudly yawning.
I ran down the stairs as happy as could be,
Because I got a new Wii,
And opened the game,
As fast as you could say my name!

I felt shocked when my guinea pigs died.
I went downstairs and cried.
Then I got some breakfast sadly,
Then I ate it quite gladly.
Then my brother took me for a ride.

Mia Hall
Oxbridge Lane Primary School, Stockton-on-Tees

Emotions Poem

I felt excited when it was Christmas and I stayed up late,
I opened my presents after eight.
We had chocolate to eat,
Until it was time for meat,
Next Christmas will be a long wait.

I felt unhappy when I had an injection,
It was as painful as an operation.
I wasn't in a hurry
Because it made me worry
Then I stayed at home and watched the television.

Rosie Partridge (9)
Oxbridge Lane Primary School, Stockton-on-Tees

Emotions Poem

I felt angry when I was struggling to use the Raspberry Pi.
I could see that the raspberry was a sign!
The Raspberry Pi was grey
But not the colour of clay!
Someone started to help me as fast as she could be!

I was excited when my Wii console was fixed
And nothing had got mixed!
The Wii is white
But not as dark at the night
But it looks as if it is the number six!

Ndumiso Ndlovu
Oxbridge Lane Primary School, Stockton-on-Tees

Emotions Poem

When I came to Oxbridge School
I thought it was cool.
I couldn't wait to start maths
And in Year 3 we went to the baths
And I listened to the golden rules.

I was sad when my great nanna died,
I thought about her and I cried.
Uncle Graeme talked about fishing,
I was listening and wishing
That I'd rather go and hide.

Aiden Binks
Oxbridge Lane Primary School, Stockton-on-Tees

Emotions Poem

I felt excited when I got a rabbit
It felt as fluffy as a carpet
I took it to the shops
And fed it Coco Pops
But it got poorly and needed the vet.

I was excited when I took my nephew to the park
We all saw a great big shark
We went on the swings
Then we went on the rings
Then the dog started to bark.

Isa Salim
Oxbridge Lane Primary School, Stockton-on-Tees

Emotions Poem

I felt joyful when I went on holiday,
We go the water park every day.
At the water park it was dark,
I felt like a swimming shark,
And my dog started to bark.

I was unhappy when my grandma and grandad died,
I couldn't believe they were one hundred and five!
I went downstairs, 'Why?' I cried,
Even though my shoelaces were untied,
I wish my grandma and grandad were alive.

Natasha Rogers
Oxbridge Lane Primary School, Stockton-on-Tees

Emotions Poem

I was joyful when I moved to Oxbridge Lane,
Even though the weather was a pain.
I was surprised,
When lots of kids arrived,
I'd love to come again.

I was nervous when I jumped in the pool,
My brain said, 'Don't be a fool!'
I swam a full length,
It took all my strength
Then I thought it was really cool.

Emily Dishi (9)
Oxbridge Lane Primary School, Stockton-on-Tees

Emotion Poem

I felt angry when my sister and I were playing tig,
She made me cross because she was wearing a big wig.
I was cross because my sister kicked me for not buying her anything
Then she pressed the button on the till and it went *ting!*
I felt excited when I got my new glasses,
I rushed back home, they weighed masses.
I felt happy when I got into cooking club,
My mam was really pleased, she wanted some nice grub.
I felt surprised when I found a pound,
It was just sitting there, on a mound.

Safaa Khaliq
Oxbridge Lane Primary School, Stockton-on-Tees

Emotions Poem

I felt joyful when Dad booked a holiday because I could swim every day,
We went for three weeks,
And jumped on some peaks,
And me and my brothers could have a play.

I was upset when my great grandma died,
I had a cuddle with Mum and cried.
I tried to stop crying
But when it turned dark I started whining.

Grace Gibson
Oxbridge Lane Primary School, Stockton-on-Tees

Emotion Poem

When I went swimming I was meeting my friend,
In the swimming pool at the end,
We both had a race, we had fun,
Then at the end we ate a bun.

On Halloween I scared the kids
In the streets they blew their lids.
I ate some sweets
And lots of treats
We collected lots of quids.

Leonardo Dogjani (9)
Oxbridge Lane Primary School, Stockton-on-Tees

Emotion Poem

My cat died, I cried,
My body felt not surprised
Then I rode my bike through the night,
Then I flew my kite last night

I felt excited when I got my new bike.
I rode it, but there was a spike,
My wheel went down
And I gave a frown.
And I saw a clown going on a hike!

Shamaar McBlain
Oxbridge Lane Primary School, Stockton-on-Tees

Emotions Poem

I am happy when I go to school
But my mum thinks I'm a fool
When I went swimming I swam in the pool
Then I played with a tool.

I was angry because you stole my book
'Where will I find it Mum?'
'Have a look'
Then she hung me on a hook
And she started to cook.

Aman Habib
Oxbridge Lane Primary School, Stockton-on-Tees

Emotions Poem

I felt angry when my friend pushed me over,
I wanted to cry and sit on the sofa.
She told me jokes to make me laugh,
Then I went home and had a bath.

I felt sad when my dog died, she was called Pip,
She used to turn our house into a tip.
We used to play ball,
Until she had fall,
Then she had a kip.

Mille-Ann Hutchinson
Oxbridge Lane Primary School, Stockton-on-Tees

Emotion Poem

I felt joyful when my mam let me play out,
And I ran all about.
So Hazal and Lilly ran into a van
And saw a man,
And we all gave a big shout.

I felt silly when my friend started to brag,
Because she was holding a brand new bag.
We had a toy that belonged to a boy,
And it smelt like an old rag.

Melisa Kirschmann (9)
Oxbridge Lane Primary School, Stockton-on-Tees

Emotions Poem

I felt excited when I went swimming with my mum at Splash,
It was as joyful as skipping with my friend Tash,
We stayed there all night, until it was light
And I went home and had a crash.

I was unhappy when I had an injection,
It was as painful as being bullied.
Mum was there to ease the tension,
They put on a plaster and I felt relieved.

Nicole Nyilika (9)
Oxbridge Lane Primary School, Stockton-on-Tees

Emotions Poem

I got hyper in my bedroom from a nightmare,
My heart was beating like at the funfair,
So we went to Smyths to buy a new toy
And I was again a happy boy.

I always get angry when my cousins mess up my room
So I always have to clean my room with a broom,
Now I am glad that my room isn't bad,
Now I can go on a hike with my dad.

Harris Ali
Oxbridge Lane Primary School, Stockton-on-Tees

Emotion Poem

I was upset when I had to go to school,
Because I thought everyone would say I was a fool.
My mam feels happy when she sits and looks at the sky,
I like to sit with her and watch the birds fly.
I felt excited when I went to Butterfly World,
They were so beautiful, especially the one that was swirled.
I was really angry when my sister learned to shade,
I rubbed it out so that it would fade!

Demi-Kaia Patridge
Oxbridge Lane Primary School, Stockton-on-Tees

Emotion Poem

I felt really sad when my dog bit my hand,
I had to go to hospital and get a band.
When I was swimming in the pool,
I felt happy that the water was cool.
I felt furious when I didn't get to go to Spain,
All because I had a really awful pain!
I felt excited when I walked into town,
Because there was a crazy, funny clown.

Adam Ali
Oxbridge Lane Primary School, Stockton-on-Tees

Emotion Poem

I felt so angry when I went to karate,
All because they were having a party.
I was scared to go to school,
I didn't want to jump in the giant swimming pool.
I was ever so happy when I won a medal in sport,
All my friends were there to give me support.
I felt surprised when I got my 25 metres,
I had to swim in litres and litres.

Rheis Stephenson
Oxbridge Lane Primary School, Stockton-on-Tees

Emotion Poem

I felt focused when I was writing a story,
I wrote all about a boy called Corey.
I felt jealous because my friend got a medal in sport,
I don't mind because I got lots of support.
I felt scared when I arrived at school,
So I jumped into the pool until I felt cool.
I felt happy when I ate the delicious cake,
I sat on the bench with it, near the beautiful lake.

Caleigh Savage
Oxbridge Lane Primary School, Stockton-on-Tees

Emotion Poem

I felt happy when I was going to Spain,
Although I did end up in lots of pain.
I felt excited when I went to karate,
It was just like a great big party.
I felt proud when I lifted my cousin onto my shoulders,
He could see the field full of giant boulders.
I felt cross when my brother and sister were hitting me,
I wish that they would just leave me be!

Mayson Swainston
Oxbridge Lane Primary School, Stockton-on-Tees

Emotions Poem

I got angry when I fell asleep early.
I woke up at 5 o'clock with my head all swirly.

I felt proud for my baby cousin, Anam.
She started walking, off like a cannon.

I got angry when it was Halloween,
Because my aunties wore a mask which made me scream.

Shiza Ahmed (9)
Oxbridge Lane Primary School, Stockton-on-Tees

Emotion Poem

I felt scared when I first started school,
Until I found an incredible pool.
I felt nervous when I first went into my class,
So had a drink of water from a clear glass.
I felt joyful when I baked a cake,
I wanted to look for more delicate food to make.
I felt excited when I won a medal,
I won a bike too, so I had a pedal.

Sana Ibrar Hussain (9)
Oxbridge Lane Primary School, Stockton-on-Tees

Emotion Poem

I felt nervous coming to school,
Not knowing if I was going to be a fool.
I felt amazed to my surprise,
I won an Xbox for a prize.
I felt guilty when I ran away,
Because I went to the shop and didn't pay!
I felt bad when my auntie died,
I was so upset, I really cried.

Brandon-Kai Dent
Oxbridge Lane Primary School, Stockton-on-Tees

POETRY EMOTIONS - County Durham & Yorkshire

Emotions Poem

I am proud of going to bed
At 7 o'clock I lay my head.

I get angry when my favourite games crashes
I feel so sad I cry through my lashes.

I get scared when my dogs jump out
And I let out a big, massive shout.

Thomas Bacon
Oxbridge Lane Primary School, Stockton-on-Tees

Emotion Poem

I felt happy when I moved house nearer the school
I had a surprise, there was a giant swimming pool!
I felt angry when I went to school
Everyone was saying that I was cruel!
I felt nervous because I got a scary book
I wasn't sure whether I should have a look!
I felt really happy when my mum got me my own pot
The only problem was that it was ever so hot!

Mia Durham
Oxbridge Lane Primary School, Stockton-on-Tees

Emotion Poem

I felt jealous when my sister got a new bed,
I was really angry, my face went red.
I felt disgusted when my mum gave me custard and jelly,
I felt so sick, it was really smelly!
I felt excited when I went swimming,
I did really well, I was winning.
I felt proud when I finished the Quran,
I went around everyone, even my nan.

Aribah Naveed
Oxbridge Lane Primary School, Stockton-on-Tees

Emotions Poem

I am proud, I biked so far.
I went further than the car.

I get angry when I fall asleep early.
I wake up at 5 o'clock with my head all swirly.

I am proud of riding my new bike to school,
I like riding my new bike because it is cool.

Markus Lawson (9)
Oxbridge Lane Primary School, Stockton-on-Tees

Emotion Poem

I felt foolish for dropping my phone,
Into a lovely ice cream cone.
I felt happy when I knew I was getting a new pet,
She arrived at my house at sunset.
I was sad when my mum got me an iPad,
I didn't want to share it with my dad.
When my mum had a baby, I felt happy,
Especially when I found out it was a chappy.

Charlie Shepherd
Oxbridge Lane Primary School, Stockton-on-Tees

Emotions Poem

I am proud of being a carer for my big sister,
You can't find no rarer.

I got angry when Harry trashed my room,
I exploded like a bomb - *boom!*

I was excited when I went to Butlins,
I went down the slippery slide,
But I cried.

Hannah Templeman (9)
Oxbridge Lane Primary School, Stockton-on-Tees

Emotions Poem

I was scared when I was in bed,
About the ghosts that were in my head,
Then I went downstairs,
For a piece of toast and I saw a ghost.

I was excited about my mother's special day,
We had fun, cake, and I said, 'Happy Anniversary Day!'

Calvin Thomas (9)
Oxbridge Lane Primary School, Stockton-on-Tees

Emotion Poems

I felt excited when I went to the fun shack,
Then I give my sister a whack.
Then I went down the slide, I had a surprise,
Then I tapped my sister on the back.

I was scared on my first Halloween, everyone was so mean.
I met a bat, then I dressed up a cat,
Then my mam dressed me up as the queen.

Lexi Bradshaw (9)
Oxbridge Lane Primary School, Stockton-on-Tees

Emotion Poem

I am a little boy that likes pizza
I got a new toy and said, 'Hallelujah!'
It was Halloween day
So I went to play
'But don't go near the neighbour!'

When I went to a circus I saw a clown
It started to juggle but I had a frown.

Brandon Cooper-Lambert (9)
Oxbridge Lane Primary School, Stockton-on-Tees

Emotion Poem

I felt happy when I got my birthday present,
To my surprise it was shaped like a crescent.
I felt excited when I was making a huge den,
I used all the sheets and cushions with help from my friend, Ben.
I felt neglected so I ran away,
But it was probably a better idea that I stay.

Katie Payne
Oxbridge Lane Primary School, Stockton-on-Tees

Emotion Poem

I felt excited when I got my pet dog,
She was so daft she tried to carry a log.
I was sad because my sister punched my back,
I was shocked that I dropped my train track.
I was so happy when I got my PS2,
I played on it all night, I didn't even go to the loo!

Jacob Richardson
Oxbridge Lane Primary School, Stockton-on-Tees

Emotion Poem

I felt happy when I got a pool,
Because everyone thought that I was really cool.
I felt jealous when my sister got a colouring book,
All I got was this silly hook!
I felt excited when I got a new toy,
My sister got one too, it was a doll called Joy!

Jannath Shahzad
Oxbridge Lane Primary School, Stockton-on-Tees

POETRY  - County Durham & Yorkshire

Emotion Poem

I felt pity when my sister got the coldest room in the house,
But it was alright, my dad bought her a pet mouse!
I felt sad when my dog passed away,
It was a very upsetting day.
I felt proud when I got my first smiley in school,
I put it on my smiley chart and it felt cool!

Scarlett Gardner
Oxbridge Lane Primary School, Stockton-on-Tees

Emotion Poem

I was happy when I made a new friend,
I knew she was someone on who I could depend.
I felt angry when my brother got new things,
I was really cross, I threw him some rings.
I felt scared when I started my new school,
I didn't want to look like a fool.

Alyssa Moody
Oxbridge Lane Primary School, Stockton-on-Tees

Emotion Poem

I felt nervous when I came to school,
Because I was going to be using a new tool.
I felt happy when I went to the fair,
Even though there were no rides there.
I felt relaxed when I went to bed.
But suddenly woke up, I hit my head!

Zain Hussain
Oxbridge Lane Primary School, Stockton-on-Tees

Emotion Poem

I felt happy when I watched a WWE fight,
But I was really glad that we were up a height.
I felt sad when my dog died,
I was so sad, I really cried.
I felt nervous when I went to the Halloween party,
When I got there I felt so arty.

Millie Lister
Oxbridge Lane Primary School, Stockton-on-Tees

Emotion Poem

I felt jealous when my mum got make-up,
Then I decided I just needed a little shake up.
I felt neglected when I ran away,
Then I decided it was best to stay.
I felt relaxed when I went on a spa day,
My mum came too, it was super, hooray!

Alisa Taylor-Hussain
Oxbridge Lane Primary School, Stockton-on-Tees

Emotion Poem

When I got to be school councillor I felt proud,
I felt like I was sat on a cloud.
I felt worried when I saw a stranger,
I called my mum because I was in danger.
I felt grumpy when it was pouring with rain,
I got very wet, it was such a pain.

Ifrah Sabaat Naveed (8)
Oxbridge Lane Primary School, Stockton-on-Tees

Emotion Poem

I felt proud when I said my first word,
My mum thought I was so clever, it was bird.
I felt angry when my brother won a medal in sport,
How could he win? He was so short!

Jake Sharp
Oxbridge Lane Primary School, Stockton-on-Tees

Emotion Poem

I felt excited when I got a new dog,
I was so happy, I took it for a jog.
When my dog had babies, I was really worried,
We went to the vet, we really hurried.

Matthew Gittins
Oxbridge Lane Primary School, Stockton-on-Tees

Emotion Poem

I felt excited when I got a cute hamster,
It was such a happy, dafty, Stockton dancer.
I felt nervous when my poorly finger was bending,
It was really sore, the pain was never-ending.

Mason Beck
Oxbridge Lane Primary School, Stockton-on-Tees

Emotion Poem

I felt nervous on my first day of school,
But after school, I went for a dip in a pool.
I was feeling sad and lonely when I was left out,
Those people were really mean, I really wanted to shout.

Bailey Plews
Oxbridge Lane Primary School, Stockton-on-Tees

What Emotion Am I?

My colour is red like lava in a bottle
I smell like lava bubbling away
My blood is blessed with lava
I taste like ghost chilli mixed with lava
It sounds like an erupting volcano in my head
I have a red dragon breathing lava into my skin and brain
I have eyes that turn red when I get outraged
I'm like a grumpy old man.

Danny Ryan (10)
Reevy Hill Primary School, Bradford

What Emotion Am I?

I'm red as blood
Everything I touch eventually dies
I taste like dead flowers
I smell like fire burning
I am a flaming volcano
I make people feel like all their good work has gone down the drain
I am the lightning in the storm
I can make the loudest roar.

Shenai Harney (9)
Reevy Hill Primary School, Bradford

What Emotion Am I?

I am purple flames but sometimes I get mixed
I taste like hot chili with lava dripping off
I smell like blood dripping off a dead body
I make a big *bang* on the landing and scream the house down, when I got angry
A volcano blows up in your body and something goes inside your body.

Leon Cunningham (9)
Reevy Hill Primary School, Bradford

What Emotion Am I?

I'm dark red, raging fire
I taste like hot chilli dying like a fly
That smells like rotten old pie.

I'm uncontrollable and I'm a flame from a spitting volcano, but why?
Which makes people feel fear and worry.
I am an exploding bomb
But who am I?

Denis Zvonovs (10)
Reevy Hill Primary School, Bradford

What Emotion Am I?

I am flaming red, the bubbles of a volcano
I taste like ghost chilli that will burn your mouth
I smell of the burning sun on a hot summer day
I am popcorn popping crazily in the microwave
I rage like a storm of lions and have a heart of stone
I make people feel like they are going to burn.

I am Anger!

Kyle Bower (9)
Reevy Hill Primary School, Bradford

What Emotion Am I?

I am the colour red like a burning fire
I taste of the hottest chilli in the world
I am a lion's roar
I smell of a hot chilli
I look like a ball of flaming fire
I am an erupting volcano bursting with fire
I feel like a ball of fire tumbling in your stomach.

Jaml Leigh Barwell (9)
Reevy Hill Primary School, Bradford

What Emotion Am I?

I smell like raging fire
I will destroy the land
I am dark red like dragon's blood
I taste like chilli dipped in lava
I attack like a fiery bullet
I am the creator of lava
Who am I?

Gavinder Bassra (9)
Reevy Hill Primary School, Bradford

What Emotion Am I?

I am red like the colour of an erupting volcano
I taste like off milk and mouldy eggs
I smell like a fire burning
I look like a fireball
I am like a fire-breathing dragon
I feel like an oven that is on.

Courtney Mclean (9)
Reevy Hill Primary School, Bradford

What Emotion Am I?

I am as red as your blood
I taste like a red-hot chilli erupting in your mouth
I smell as bad as raging fire
I sound as loud as a fire-breathing dragon
I feel like blood boiling inside
I look like a volcano erupting.

Harrison Lee Windsor (9)
Reevy Hill Primary School, Bradford

What Emotion Am I?

I am flaming red like an erupting volcano
I taste like the fiery sun on a sunny day
I am popcorn exploding in the sky
I am a raging lion

I am Anger!

Phoebe Powell (9)
Reevy Hill Primary School, Bradford

POETRY  - County Durham & Yorkshire

What Emotion Am I?

I am the colour red like dark red blood
I taste like out of date milk and rotten eggs
I sound like a loud firework in the sky
I look small with fire on my head
I am like a volcano bubbling.

Codie Regan (9)
Reevy Hill Primary School, Bradford

What Emotion Am I?

I am a dragon who breathes red fire
I taste like chillies from small seeds
I am a black volcano with strange lava
I smell like burning bread
So who am I?

Sarah
Reevy Hill Primary School, Bradford

What Is Anger?

I am the colour dark red, like streaming blood
I taste like burning chillies cooking in an overheated oven
I smell like a flaming hot fire burning lots of rubber
It makes a weird crackling noise in your ear.

Lawson Hammond
Reevy Hill Primary School, Bradford

What Emotion Am I?

I am a burning red volcano
I taste as hot as a chilli
I sound like a rhino charging towards you
I am Anger.

Ebony Cleworth (9)
Reevy Hill Primary School, Bradford

Let Her Go

Sad is like a song.
'Let Her Go' is sad to me.
When Nanna Bid died

Sad had grey hair and glasses
down on her nose

Sad is memories, I miss my
Nanna Bid and Grandad Hughie

Memories make me cry
They make my nose runny
And tears drop down

And I still think nice thoughts about
Nanna Bid and Grandad Hughie.

Sam Stewart (10)
Riverside School, Goole

Sadness In The Dark

There is no gasoline to my flame, no spring in my step
They say sadness is blue but yet I cannot see colour in the world.
The stench of rotten meat is forever in the air, it is the stench of sadness.
It sounds like screams and crying
It always stays in my ear.
It feels like ice.
But yet I am destined to walk alone and sad.

Kofi Fricker (10)
Riverside School, Goole

Sad

Sad sounds like screaming,
It tastes like snot down the throat,
It smells like hot steam (melting pumpkins).
Sadness is red,
It looks like a hairdryer,
Sadness feels like broken glass.
Mean people make me sad.

Luke Dowse (10)
Riverside School, Goole

Happy At The Fair

Happy is green
It tastes like ice cream
And smells like Hull fair
Happy looks like a doggy
The sound of a song
Happy feels like tickling.

Ehsan Mann (10)
Riverside School, Goole

Happy

Happy is the colour blue,
It looks like smiling zebras, singing children and fluffy clouds in the blue sky.
It tastes like strawberries and smells like sweets.
Happiness is the sound of music and feels soft.
Happiness is the love from my mum.

Beth Sims (10)
Riverside School, Goole

Fear

Fear is purple.
It tastes like broccoli.
And smells like carrots.
Fear looks like bats.
The sound of shivers.
Fear feels like spiders.

Oliver Goulsbra Miller (10)
Riverside School, Goole

A Happy Poem

Happy is blue and green
Happy tastes like Haribos.
It smells like red and green apples.
Happy looks like you are joyful.
It sounds like you are giggly and it feels like you are excited.

Connor Parkinson (10)
Riverside School, Goole

Thomas The Tank Is Green To Me

Excitement is the colour of green.
Excitement feels like happiness to me.
Excitement tastes like green apples.
Excitement sounds like train engines running
It smells like the steam from the train's chimney.

Jack Gardner (9)
Riverside School, Goole

Happy

Happy is glowing yellow,
Happy smells like sausages and sounds like someone resting.
Happiness looks like a ginger flying person travelling over America.
Happiness is the end of the day, school bell ringing, it's time to go home.

Reece Dunn (9)
Riverside School, Goole

Sadness

Tears taste like salt as salty as the salty sea.
It looks like your father died in the ocean.
It feels like water dripping through you.
Sadness sounds like screams of help from the distance.

Reece McCrory (9)
Riverside School, Goole

Happy

Happy is the colour blue.
Happy smells like flowers and tastes like sweet apples.
Happiness feels like a big smile on my face.
I am happy when I am at school.

Mia Cunningham (10)
Riverside School, Goole

Sadness

Today I feel sad,
I don't know why,
But I'm really upset,
I want to cry.

The tears are flowing,
Down my face,
I feel like I'm part,
Of an emotional case.

I'm a little bit angry,
I want to be alone,
What is the matter? I want to know.

I feel down and so upset,
My life is beginning to be a dread,
Maybe it's school? I just don't know.

Now I've spoken to someone,
I'm relieved and happy,
That the job is done,
I'm not upset, I don't want to cry,
Even though I don't know why,
I feel happy deep down inside.

Georgia Thompson (10)
Throston Primary School, Hartlepool

When I Am Angry

When I am angry I like to fight
I might get sent to my room
When I am angry I get told off
My mam brushed the floor with a broom
When I am angry I sit in my bedroom upset
My room gets in a mess
When I am angry I hit hard
I might go mad

When I am angry I get shouted at
I might go mad
When I am angry I don't care
I hate being angry

When I am angry I get in a mess
I like to get angry, I do it a lot
When I am angry I do nothing in my room
I don't like to get angry anymore which I am happy about.

When I am angry I like to run to my room to calm down!

Ryan McAllister
Throston Primary School, Hartlepool

Christmas

Christmas, what a brilliant thing
Let the Christmas bells ring
First, we'll set up the tree
My mum will do it, with help from me
Then we'll pick up my family
After, we'll open our presents happily
Then we'll scoff our delicious dinner
And then we'll do a race, I hope I'm the winner
Then we'll play with all our toys
After we'll say bye-bye to the boys
Then we'll play some girly games
Then I look out the windowpanes
I hope it's snowing
Yes, my grandma's going!
Then we go and play in the snow
My dad comes home and says, 'Ho, ho, ho!'
Oh Christmas time I cannot lie
I do not want to say goodbye.

Maddie Trueman-Wray (9)
Throston Primary School, Hartlepool

The Difference Between Joy And Sadness

Sometimes I feel sad,
And I get wet in the rain,
Sometimes I am mad,
Then I feel a pain,
But all the while,
I will try to smile!

Joy is something I share with the world,
I look in a tree and see a centipede,
I smile as around my finger it curls,
And joy is here to back up my needs,
For anyone will do good deeds!

Sadness is something I barely feel,
I love to ride my bike!
I get sad when I'm all alone,
But not when I'm at home!

Tegan Tunstall (9)
Throston Primary School, Hartlepool

Joyful

My joy is my birthday and the colour of blue,
When the party is over I always say, 'Phew!'
It looks like a sunny day and I always lay on the grass
So soon and so fast.
Smell of the air like I have spiky hair.
It is so good and so nice,
So quick and so fast.
All of it is like a dash and the birds tweeting in a gap.
When I am on a farm I always eat ham and bacon
And it is so nice.
The feel of my bed until it is in my head
When that happens before I read.

Ethan Kinnersley (7)
Throston Primary School, Hartlepool

Times And Emotions

I'm happy in the day,
I don't spend the day sighing in dismay

I'm angry in the night
When the sky is bright

I'm bored at lunch
Because I prefer brunch

I feel foolish in the morning
Because I'm still snoring
I feel smart when I'm at school
But not when I'm in the pool.

Jay Nicholson (9)
Throston Primary School, Hartlepool

Christmas Time Is Here!

C ake is cool when I eat it up,
H appy, joyful, I can't get to sleep,
R ipping my presents and seeing what's inside,
I thank my parents and hug them tight,
S till can't repay them for all their gifts,
T *ick-tock*, can I go outside,
M aking snowmen and winning the race,
A nd then a snowball fight,
S till haven't told you it's my birthday on Christmas Day!

B est of all,
I t's double the gifts,
R unning to the couch, then I'm out of breath,
T hen I lie down and think about the world,
H appy world and grateful me, can't wait till the bunny's come,
D on't you know the Birthday Bear?
A nd the Easter Bunny too?
Y ou do believe in Christmas magic, don't you?

Emily-Kate Brown (10)
Throston Primary School, Hartlepool

Happiness

Happiness is a feeling that makes people smile,
Winning makes you feel joyful and excited,
When you're happy you're not sad or mad, so you can be glad.

When you're proud you're happy and believing,
So all you want to do is be grateful and keep receiving,
Progressing on, you know you're achieving.

Goals accomplished to make things right,
At first it was quite a fight,
But now I know I've finally done it,
Now I feel like I've reached the summit.

Sam Codner (10)
Throston Primary School, Hartlepool

Happiness

Happiness is a joyful yellow
Sadness is a deep, dark blue
Anger is a ruby red
Fear is a lilac purple
Happiness lives inside me
Sadness grows all around
Anger is a devilish demon
Fear lies inside and out.
My nana is like sadness
My grandad is like anger
My rabbit is like fear
And I'm just like joy.

Ellie May Ashley (10)
Throston Primary School, Hartlepool

Happiness

Happiness is the best feeling,
It feels very good,
But when the tear monster came,
I did the best I could.

I was starting to cry,
But happiness fought back,
I now see rainbows,
Instead of seeing black.

Now I'm floating through the sky,
Seeing rainbows and birds that fly,
Happiness is a feeling in me and you,
Looking around, what a beautiful view!

I'm now feeling not as blue,
There is something I want to tell you,
I am happy, so are you,
Happy is an emotion, you should feel it too!

Ben Mills (10)
Throston Primary School, Hartlepool

Emotions

Happiness is bright yellow,
it makes me feel best,
it smells like marshmallows,
I never want it to rest.

Anger is dark red,
it makes me feel stressed,
I like to pull off a pencil lead,
when it's over my room is all messed.

Sad is light blue,
I cry all night long,
my mum is sad too,
I feel like singing a depressed song.

Boredom is dark grey,
for when I have nothing to do,
there on the floor I lay,
I'd just lay at home too!

Tabitha McQuilling (9)
Throston Primary School, Hartlepool

What Emotion Am I?

My hands are shaking
Shaking with fear
Running from
A monster with terrible ears
Jaws are chomping
Chomping like mad
I'm scared to bits
Please don't make me sad
What emotion am I?

Answer: Fear.

Eve Black (8)
Throston Primary School, Hartlepool

The Mysterious Anger

Anger is spooky, it's a freaky thing inside your body.
When you're in the house check where you are because Anger can't keep inside.
When you're in bed face the wall, don't turn your head because Anger will be there.

It sleeps in a cave,
It's scary as can be,
When it comes out the cave,
It can destroy you.

So when you're walking in the streets,
Be careful where you go,
Because you never know,
Anger could be there.

Vinny Rowbotham (9)
Throston Primary School, Hartlepool

Happiness

Happiness is the best feeling,
Seeing rainbows as bright as the sun,
Loving life - never looking back - hoping that I won.

When you're happy nothing can bring you down,
You want to tell the world,
You want to scream with joy.

It's easy to be positive when you're happy,
Lots of things to say,
Spreading the message, smiling more makes me happier every day.

Beth Williamson (10)
Throston Primary School, Hartlepool

How I Feel

Sometimes I feel happy,
Sometimes I feel blue,
Sometimes I feel friendly,
How about you?

Sometimes I'm determined,
Sometimes I feel fear,
Sometimes I'm scared of things
and I won't dare to go near.

Sometimes I feel anxious,
Sometimes I feel guilt,
Sometimes I feel proud,
of a structure I've built.

Sometimes I feel creeped,
Sometimes I feel mad,
Sometimes I feel joy,
but I always feel glad.

Will Tighe (9)
Throston Primary School, Hartlepool

Sadness

I started the day all cheerful,
but I ended the day all tearful.
Tomorrow is Monday and my parents are shouting hip, hip hooray!
As it's back to school,
because the next day is Monday.
I try to put a smile upon my face,
but when I am with my friend I'm in a darker place.

Singing of the birds make me cry
Another day of sadness ahead of me
Darting down my face, tears stream down me.

Ellie Jade Kelsey (10)
Throston Primary School, Hartlepool

Fierce

I'm a fierce tiger
If I want someone I'll find her
I'm going to get you
Stay still, 'Boo!'
I'm ready to pound
Shh, don't make a sound
I'm fierce and not scared
Fierce is what they call me
This is my life story.

Don't annoy me, you'll learn
I'll bite, I'll scratch, I'll roar, sometimes I'll really claw
I'm fierce and not scared, I can do it
Don't get me angry, not a little bit.

I live in a dark cave, when I'm around you're not safe.
Fierce is what they call me.
You really shouldn't ignore me.

Faith Evans (9)
Throston Primary School, Hartlepool

What Makes Me Infuriated

Being infuriated feels ignorant
I don't like it
Sometimes fear makes me pant
Just a bit

I am fearless
I'm not scared
I do get stressed
Sometimes I'm first

Being enraged
Feels bad
Plus being outraged
There again, I'm always mad!

Kai Arnold (9)
Throston Primary School, Hartlepool

Anger!

Angry, angry, why, why, why?
Angry, angry, I want to cry.

Angry, angry, I feel mad,
Angry, angry, I feel sad.

Angry, angry, slamming my door,
Angry, angry, throwing things on my floor.

Angry, angry, I am glad,
Angry, angry, I'm not mad.

Mrs Angry has gone to bed,
Now it is time to lie down my head.

Happy, happy, it comes at the end
Happy, happy, it's always round the bend.

Sad, sad, as this poem has come to an end,
Sad, sad, see you later my old friend.

Charlotte Scott (10)
Throston Primary School, Hartlepool

Happiness Is A Wonderful Thing

Once there was a girl who was happy as can be
She saw love and happiness in all that she would see
She was always smiling with her happy little face
She was possibly the happiest girl in the whole human race.

But once there was a little girl who was oh so very sad
And because of that she acted oh so very bad
But when she met the happy girl the sadness washed away
And she became happier every single day.

Happiness is a wonderful thing
It can wash away sadness with the good that it will bring
So always be joyful and never be depressed
Because that way your life will be better than the rest.

Lucy White (10)
Throston Primary School, Hartlepool

Happy As Laughter

Happy is nice, happy is cool
Happy is good when you're not a fool
Happy goes on all day long
Happiness fills the world with smiles and it will stay like that for a while.

H appy is laughter, happy is true all the time through
A ll around the Ferris wheel, laughter goes on all around the wheel
P arties you dance, parties you cheer, together we're here
P artners we help, partners we explore, partners we help to get new goals
Y ou and me, best friends now, together forever and fun time we'll have.

The way we live happiness will be here forever long, cheer, laughter from your house.
Cheerful games for us all to play.

Daniel Hill (10)
Throston Primary School, Hartlepool

Anger Rocks!

A nger hides deep inside
N ot only his power is wide
G iving people bad words
E mpty heart and he is a conqueror of worlds
R iding on fire, being so strong

A nd his claws are big and long
N othing but an empty soul
G iving people bad messages and sending meteors to make holes
E nding worlds that made him banished
R iding on fire with hair so wild.

Alex Trotter (9)
Throston Primary School, Hartlepool

Feelings Are Nice

F rightened is my worst feeling of all
E ven when I see a spider I fall
E xcited is the best, it is at the top
L istening to the wrapping paper it will never stop
I nvestigating makes me feel cool
N othing will beat it, except my boring school
G rateful is nice but not the best
S ometimes I love a present but it isn't to the test

A ngry is bad, I hate it so much
R aiding through the fridge, then I get the touch
E very feeling is nice, except anger, it is not the best

N o one knows about this feeling except from me
I want to tell you it is hungry
C ruel is not nice for when you are picked on
E very day if I get angry I go to Mr Atkinson.

Lucie Griffith (9)
Throston Primary School, Hartlepool

Things I Hate!

When someone annoys me,
When someone kicks me,
Oh, it makes me angry,
And everyone hates me.

If I can't play on my PS3,
It really annoys me,
Same with the Wii,
It makes me angry!

When I can't see a movie,
You couldn't just guess,
Or maybe you could,
It makes me angry!
These are things that make me angry!

Jacob George Carney (9)
Throston Primary School, Hartlepool

Sadness!

Sadness fills the air,
It's such a nightmare,
The sky is full of rain clouds so
You do not feel proud,
When you are sad!

The sky is all dark,
Like an empty park,
You feel lonely,
You're even moany,
When you are sad!

Tears pour down your face,
You're in a dark place,
You're white as a sheet,
You can't deal with the heat,
When you're sad!

Louie Brown (10)
Throston Primary School, Hartlepool

Happiness

H appiness is the best
A nd I feel better than the rest
P lease help me feel happiness
P eople around the world have different feelings too
I like happiness when I'm happy
N early everyday I'm put to the test, even though happiness is the best
E ven if you're sad, happiness makes you better
S adness is horrible, happy is cool as a rule
S ometimes there's different feelings too.

Harry Huntley (9)
Throston Primary School, Hartlepool

Sad

When the tears swell up,
Right inside of you,
Your eyes go all red,
When you're feeling blue,
Your nose starts to tingle,
And your heart goes all tight,
Now it is time for you to go and fight.

Tears drip down your face,
And fall onto the ground,
They splash into puddles,
As sadness is all around,
The blackness fills the skies,
As I suffocate in tears,
The skies slowly clear,
And so do my fears.

Katie Pattison (10)
Throston Primary School, Hartlepool

Happiness

H ip, hip hooray! It will be a great day today,
A great sigh of relief is what I feel,
P artying is what I do,
P izza is what I eat,
I n the house I watch TV,
N ice and fresh is what I feel,
E spaña is where I want to go,
S ipping my drink is what I do,
S lurping down my food is how I eat.

Daniel Arnell (10)
Throston Primary School, Hartlepool

Delighted

It is always nice to be delighted
It is nice when you go to places
You feel delighted when you win an award
You feel delighted when you win a match

You feel amazed if you win a football match
You feel happy if it's your birthday or Christmas
You feel delighted if you go on holiday
It is nice to know you're delighted

It's always nice to be joyful
When going on a summer adventure
A present that you are delighted with

These things make you delighted
You win an award and are proud of yourself
It's always nice to be happy.

Ben Green (9)
Throston Primary School, Hartlepool

24 Hours In The Freeze!

Sometimes I feel scared and I feel all cold
I feel I can't control it, it's not in my mind
My body freezes, I shiver with fear
I feel I'm going to die
My body's shaking fast
Can I stop it? I feel I can't
I try not to worry even though it's hard
What emotion am I?

Answer: Terrified.

Aidan Howe (8)
Throston Primary School, Hartlepool

Clueless

Clueless is bright white
He crawls through the night
Searching for answers
He tastes like prancers
Dancing inside me
Sometimes he can't see
The answers in my book
He just doesn't bother to look!

He's always banging in my head
He never lets me sleep in bed
Sometimes he's even said
'You go to sleep
And I won't make a peep!'

But I don't trust him!

Naomi Park-Hanson (10)
Throston Primary School, Hartlepool

Happiness

H appiness makes the world a better place
A lways try your best to be happy
P ractical jokes can make your friends happy
P eople everywhere try their best to be happy
I n your dreams you're always happy
N ever be sad
E very day you should be happy
S adness is horrible
S ummer makes me feel happy.

Mollie Jenkins (10)
Throston Primary School, Hartlepool

Happiness And Joy

Happiness makes me smile.
Happiness makes me think of happy thoughts.
Happiness makes me cool.
Happiness makes me love.
Happiness feels like hugs.
Happiness makes me joyful.
Happiness makes me calm.
Happiness smells like lavender.
Happiness sounds like birds.

Lara Ann Stewart (7)
Throston Primary School, Hartlepool

Happy

Happy is the best feeling
It improves your mood a lot
I always share my happiness
to all and everyone
People say my joyful spirit
Can always cheer you up
At the end of the day
I always say . . .
be happy for what you have got.

Trinity Bowman (10)
Throston Primary School, Hartlepool

Happiness

H ow happiness helps me through the day
A chance to drive all the sad away
P ut a smile on your face
P ut a stop to all disgrace
I t's truly the best
N ever doing a test
E verything I love so much
S o make happiness a smiley touch,
S o happiness is the best by far!

Isabel Hodgson (10)
Throston Primary School, Hartlepool

Anger

A rguing with my family
N ervous for tomorrow
G rounded in my bedroom
E yes popping out
R ipping up sheets, what am I doing?

Slamming doors
Stamping my feet
Smashing windows.

Amy Burton (11)
Throston Primary School, Hartlepool

Love

F ondness means love
O ver the hills flies a dove
N obody knows my secret crush
D espite that he's amazingly lush
N othing can distract me from him
E veryone knows that he's very slim
S o even if he's as far away as a mile
S tanding, he still sees my beautiful smile!

Laura Jukes-Bell (9)
Throston Primary School, Hartlepool

Anger

O pposite of calm, out of control
U nder control is now what it is
T his little creature comes with no warning
R aging and kicking its hobby
A rguing and shouting is what it does best
G ritting my teeth is the actions it likes
E nemies with happiness
D evil is its boss.

Travis Gorton (9)
Throston Primary School, Hartlepool

Nervous

Before I go onstage,
I get a nervous rage,
Then what do I do?
I find someone to talk to,
Then they keep me calm,
So I wipe my sweaty palm,
Then I am fine,
Why do I get nervous?

Libbie Frostick (10)
Throston Primary School, Hartlepool

Happiness

Happiness is as happy as a pug that is blue
It tastes like the most tastiest chocolate you have ever tasted
It smells like the most scrumptious marshmallows that you have wasted
It looks like a smile that you have pasted
It sounds like someone is giggling
It feels like someone is tickling you.

Sammy Dhaliwal (9)
Throston Primary School, Hartlepool

Joyful

The colour is yellow.
Joy is my birthday and the colour of yellow.
When the party is over I always say, 'Finally!'
It looks like a rainy day and I always like to stay in bed.
It smells like strawberry cream.
When I am happy I can always hear the birds tweeting.
When I feel happy the grass is always near my feet.
I look like a princess.

Lucy Burton (8)
Throston Primary School, Hartlepool

Emotions, Emotions, Emotions

I am happy
When I try
I am cheerful
When I fly
I am joyful
When it snows
I am light-hearted
When I glow.

Lucy Jasmine Agar (8)
Throston Primary School, Hartlepool

Anger

Anger is red like lava
It tastes like spicy peppers which makes steam come out of your ears
It smells like spicy peppers which make your eyes water
It looks like an erupting volcano raining lava
It sounds like groaning people
It feels like dynamite ready to blow in your head.

Patrick Bainbridge (8)
Throston Primary School, Hartlepool

Anger

Anger is red like fiery lava
It tastes like red-hot lava which burns your hands off
It smells like a forest burning to the ground with toxic smoke rising from the forest
It looks like a red man with evil red eyes and an angry grin, as well as very hot flames coming out of his head
It sounds like animal meat crisping
It feels like it's making me happy by letting my rage out.

Jonathan Stamper (8)
Throston Primary School, Hartlepool

Shyness

It's a new school year, don't know how to act,
As fast as a cheetah I run to class.
The new maths teacher fires a question,
8 x 9
don't know, can't find, the answer is around,
Once again I've been put on the spot,
Then all of a sudden it comes to me,
72! Correct!

Alyssa Suggitt (10)
Throston Primary School, Hartlepool

Happiness

Happy is a light purple
It tastes like melted marshmallows
Happy smells like beautiful sunflowers
Happy looks like a love heart
Happy sounds like a violin
Happy cuddles me tightly
Happy lives in my heart.

Summer Elizabeth Inglesant (9)
Throston Primary School, Hartlepool

Football

F ootball is the best!
O h yes, it's gonna be the best and beat all the rest
O h, everyone loves football
T o the pitch we go kicking balls on the go
B alls to kick, balls to catch all over the place
A t home we play football, we also play at school
L ike football, absolutely love scoring goals!
L ove good saves, love good goals.

Ben Eglintine (9)
Throston Primary School, Hartlepool

Mr Fear

When Mr Fear is unleashed
He seems to control the chills up my back
Mr Fear magically makes butterflies dance in my belly
I have to run away, I can't blow him away
He comes out like a flash
All jumpy and shaky like jelly
When he makes me fiddle I could scream!
When Mr Fear is unleashed.

Molly McPartlin (10)
Throston Primary School, Hartlepool

Happiness Is . . .

Happiness lurks in the candyfloss meadows
Where the ice cream bunnies of positivity glow
Happiness is a light dreamy gold
A warm toasty feeling, the opposite of cold
When your mouth creeps into a frown
It never takes long to turn it upside down
Happiness is the best by far!

Maddie Smith
Throston Primary School, Hartlepool

What Emotion Am I?

My hands feel all wrinkly and sweaty
My face is drizzled with dark blue tears
My eyes are bulging with tremendous fear
But my mouth is as moistureless as a crumbly, rocky cliff side
I feel so faint my head is in terrible agony
What emotion am I?

Answer: Sadness.

Sophie Pattison (8)
Throston Primary School, Hartlepool

Don't Be Nervous

N ervous is my emotion
E very day it's a commotion
R eally it stops me from doing most things, it feels like a curse
V iolent things make me feel worse
O bviously they do
U nder the bush I sit all day, I wish I had someone like you
S o I sit all day in dismay.

Tegan Smith (9)
Throston Primary School, Hartlepool

Disgust

The colour of disgust is green
Because she doesn't like green vegetables.
I can see green, horrible, yucky, disgusting grass.
I can feel horrible, bursting, yucky green vegetables.
I smell horrible wet fossils.
I hear the noise of people shouting.
I taste green, yucky vegetables.

Lucy Thompson (7)
Throston Primary School, Hartlepool

Joy

Joy is light blue like fluffy candyfloss
It tastes like a cake
It smells like lovely flowers with awesome powers
It looks like the greatest person in the world
It sounds like a huge wave that is crashing on the beach's shore
It feels like you're never going to be alone and you've got a friend in your arms.

Keira Vaughan (8)
Throston Primary School, Hartlepool

My Dog

My dog looks like a puppy.
My dog feels fluffy.
My dog smells like flowers.
My dog is black and white.
My dog sounds like a tiger.
My dog is the best!
This is my joy and happiness.

Amber Arnell (7)
Throston Primary School, Hartlepool

Sadness

S adness is the worst feeling to have
A nd it always makes me think of bad things that's happened
D oing nothing but just being sad and crying
N othing is worse than sadness
E ven being angry
S adness is worse than anything else
S o don't be sad!

Luke Steven Swales (10)
Throston Primary School, Hartlepool

Anger

Anger is as dark red as a bloodshot moon
It tastes like terrible, horrible onions that make your eyes water
It smells like lion's teeth that have never been brushed
It looks like a big, massive, red juicy apple
It sounds like a massive bookshelf crashing to the ground
It feels like a humongous bomb planted inside your stomach ready to explode.

Rhys Denton (8)
Throston Primary School, Hartlepool

Happiness!

H appiness fills your body today
A ll your anger floats away
P eople laughing and giggling too
P uppies dancing and prancing around, singing their song and panting about
Y our everlasting laughter which makes you want to cry. So just have fun and enjoy your day because happiness is coming right your way.

Amber Gavillet (10)
Throston Primary School, Hartlepool

Anger

The colours of anger are red, black and grey.
Anger makes me look like thunder and tornadoes.
Anger smells like a big fire and a bomb exploding and people smoking.
Anger sounds like people stomping and people screaming.
When I'm angry I feel I'm in Anger Town
And with angry people who punch and fight and scream.

Joshua Flint (7)
Throston Primary School, Hartlepool

Sadness

Everybody makes me frown, every day I want my mummy.
Nobody lets me play with them, all I want is a good friend.
Every time I see someone playing I always think, what am I doing?
Every time I ask people if I could play they always ignore me and run away.
I always feel a tear dropping down my face
When I see them talking and running away.

Grace Butt (7)
Throston Primary School, Hartlepool

Happy

H appy is me.
A pples and grapes make me great.
P opop says, 'Look at me, I'm free!'
P ools is my favourite team.
Y ellow is my favourite colour.

This is what happiness means to me.

Leo Rooke (7)
Throston Primary School, Hartlepool

Anger

Anger, the flashing, red fire.
I smell the smell of smoke burning.
I taste the taste of broccoli.
I hear people shouting at each other.
I see the horrible grazes on people's knees.
I feel the horrible rocks on the ground.

Sam Mills (7)
Throston Primary School, Hartlepool

Anger

Anger is red like a juicy tomato
It tastes like a rotten grown apple which will make you sick
It smells like red-hot burning fire which will burn your veins
It looks like a dark red that will make you sick
It sounds like a roar from a big lion
It feels like a red-hot burning fire which will bring you to your death.

Milly Smith (8)
Throston Primary School, Hartlepool

The Anger Monster

A t the trash can, round the corner is where he lives
N ow and then usually he comes out to frighten children
and make them cry
G o indoors because Anger can't keep inside
E very day he horrifies twenty children
R ound the corner of the house beware or you will get snuck up on

Zachary Unthank (9)
Throston Primary School, Hartlepool

Happiness

Happiness is yellow just like bananas.
Happiness tastes like some fruit.
Happiness smells like tropical fruits.
Happiness looks like some scrummy chocolate.
Happiness sounds like relaxing music.
Happiness feels like lovely bunny rabbits.

Alfie Hastings (8)
Throston Primary School, Hartlepool

Happiness Is Brilliant

Happy is a bright yellow
It tastes like ice cream and cake
And it smells like delicious chocolate
Happy looks like a sunny day
The sound is beautiful like birds cheeping, hooray
Happy sets me free and keeps me going.

Jacob Lamb (9)
Throston Primary School, Hartlepool

Sadness

Sadness is as blue as the sky.
I see clouds, rain, thunder and lightning.
I feel the sadness inside of you.
I smell all the disgusting food on the floor.
I hear all the wet rain splashing in the puddles.
I taste all my tears dripping into my mouth.

Lilly King (7)
Throston Primary School, Hartlepool

POETRY EMOTIONS - County Durham & Yorkshire

Anger

Anger is like a burning fire
It tastes like boiling smoke in your mouth
It smells like a volcano's ash cloud
It sounds so grumpy it might explode
It looks like a red face
Anger is like a burning fire.

Ashley Grant (8)
Throston Primary School, Hartlepool

Happy!

Yellow reminds me of happiness.
Unicorns and pretty perfect things.
Looking at Candyland, it smells like perfume and spray.
I just love May, also beautiful things.
Feeling grass, sun and love that comes every day.
I just love the blue sky lying on pretty clouds.

Isabelle Elizabeth Barron (7)
Throston Primary School, Hartlepool

Anger

A nger is what I dislike
N o I really dislike it
G eez, he is not my mate
E verybody dislikes it just a bit
R emember, nobody likes it because it makes you mad like a raging bull.

Benjamin Barker (10)
Throston Primary School, Hartlepool

Joyful

J unk food is not very nice
O n top of the lightning strike
Y awn, yawn, have some
F un, even though we get our work done
U nderstand feelings of me
L oving feelings inside of me.

Alfie Johnson (9)
Throston Primary School, Hartlepool

Joyful

J elly and ice cream, mmm . . .
O pen the door full of delight
Y es, summertime!
F ull of lovely smells
U mbrellas are no good for summertime, ha
L aying down in the summer breeze makes me happy.

Alivia Crinnion (10)
Throston Primary School, Hartlepool

Fear

Fear is grey like an Xbox controller
It tastes like a green sprout
It smells like the bathroom when my dad has been in
It looks like my sister
Fear sounds like a whiteboard being scratched
Fear is grey like an Xbox controller.

Sonnie Crosman (8)
Throston Primary School, Hartlepool

Lonely

Lonely is red like a bright red crisp packet
It smells like apple pie on the windowsill, it makes me hungry
It tastes of old air up above
Lonely is echoing, gloomy footsteps
It looks like empty streets and cannot see
Lonely is red like a bright red crisp packet.

Elise-Jo Stallard (8)
Throston Primary School, Hartlepool

Disgust

Green, disgusting dark colour
Feel the disgusting wet dog
Hear the horrible squeaky sound of a recorder
Smell the horrid burnt toast
See the disgusting dead spider
Taste the horrid pear.

Izabel Madison Balch (7)
Throston Primary School, Hartlepool

Excited

Excited is pink like a perfect pig
It is popcorny, it is sweeter than sugar
It smells like cakes coming out of the oven
Excited is screaming like a baby crying
It is as smiley as the sunshine on a summer's day
Excited is pink like a perfect pig.

Billy Littlewood (8)
Throston Primary School, Hartlepool

Upset

Upset is a gloomy, grey goose on a dark day
It tastes like salty tears dropping from your eyes
It smells like pooey things on the floor
Upset is quiet and lonely, you can hear a single tear
It looks like a dark and murky day at Christmas
Upset is a gloomy, grey goose on a dark day.

Martha Kidd (8)
Throston Primary School, Hartlepool

Anger

Anger is a red bull raging
Anger is fire flickering away in the night
Anger tastes like really sour sweets
Anger is a sound that deafens us
Anger is a cheetah chasing me around my head
Anger is never asleep, he's always awake.

Macey Fleetham-Reid (9)
Throston Primary School, Hartlepool

Anger

Anger is red like an angry novel
It tastes like a hot, fiery chicken
It smells like a fireball
It looks like a hot-red flame
It sounds like a roaring lion
It feels like a flaming ball.

Rebecca Lynn (8)
Throston Primary School, Hartlepool

Joy

Joy is light blue like the sky
It tastes like the best chocolate cake
It smells like sweeties that have just been opened
It's like a happy, playful street
It sounds like church bells ringing
It feels like playing with your best friends.

Richard Andrew Barker (8)
Throston Primary School, Hartlepool

Animals

Animals make me happy.
To me animals smell like perfume.
I like animals, they're really cuddly.
To me animals feel like fluffy clouds.
Animals look really cute to me.
Animals are the best to me!

Viktoria Cooke (7)
Throston Primary School, Hartlepool

Disgust

Disgust - as green as rotten, old cabbage.
Smells as disgusting as a dirty, old farm.
Tastes as horrid as a bitter pie.
Hear a squeaking, annoying mouse.
Touch a horrible slimy frog.
See a horrid piece of sick broccoli!

Lizzy Wilson (7)
Throston Primary School, Hartlepool

Lonely

Lonely is black like bumpy coal
It is like dirty water from a filthy river
Lonely is like smoke from black ash clouds
It sounds like silence so you can hear a teardrop
Lonely means you look as if you have broken your heart
Lonely is like bumpy coal.

Emily Alton (8)
Throston Primary School, Hartlepool

Joyful

J oy makes me happy
O tters make me smile
Y our mum makes me laugh
F un makes me joyful
U p in the sky there is the sun that makes me excited
L ollipops make me feel awesome.

Jakelynd Khan (9)
Throston Primary School, Hartlepool

Anger

As black as Batman's cape,
When I see my worst enemy,
When I hear a really fast car,
When I feel a slug's slime,
When I smell asparagus,
When I taste blood.

Nathan Jensen (7)
Throston Primary School, Hartlepool

Joy

Yellow as the bright sun.
To smell the sweet, soft flowers.
To feel the thick, green grass.
To see the bright park.
To hear the birds tweeting in the distance.
To taste the sweet apple.

Taylor Crompton (7)
Throston Primary School, Hartlepool

Anger Poem

A nger is what I hate
N early going to burst
G etting ready to punch
E veryone gets angry
R eally hate my friends when I get angry.

Courtney Kennedy (10)
Throston Primary School, Hartlepool

Anger Never Lies

A nger is a beast waiting to pounce
N ever-ending words make me get annoyed
G rinning, I hate it, it makes me lash out
E veryone fears my great strength
R eflect me, I hate you!

Daniel Foster (9)
Throston Primary School, Hartlepool

Anger

A nger is one of the worst
N o one likes it because it reminds me of
G rey, which is a colour I don't like, I wish it was
E rased, even my dog
R over wishes it, so does everyone, it is true.

Carson Ibbotson (10)
Throston Primary School, Hartlepool

Anger

Anger is grey like a goose
Anger tastes like boiling red chillies on your tongue
It smells like fire inside of you
It sounds like crackles and bangs
Anger is like a big bull.

Owen Robson (8)
Throston Primary School, Hartlepool

Anger All Around

A nger is never the way to solve a problem
N ever use anger if you want to solve 'em
G reat to unleash if you're playing a video games
E ven though Anger is full of shame
R ise Anger up to your very shame, even though it is quite lame.

Jacob Luke Robinson (9)
Throston Primary School, Hartlepool

Upset

Upset is a gloomy, gliding goose from the lake
It tastes like a core from an apple from a kid's packed lunch
They smell like a rotten pie that hasn't been washed in a year
It seems like an upset girl that is soaking her hair
Upset is a gloomy, gliding goose from the lake.

Tionne Jane Wyness (9)
Throston Primary School, Hartlepool

Anger

A nger is really horrible
N ext you will be insane
G et it out your head
E verything will be superior
R ed will be gone forever!

Ben Alderson (10)
Throston Primary School, Hartlepool

Joy

Joy is the colour yellow like the shining bright sun.
Joy looks like graceful ice skating.
Joy tastes like juicy red strawberries.
Joy, I hear talking about a swimming pool.
Joy smells lovely, like cooked sausages.

Tahlia Smith (7)
Throston Primary School, Hartlepool

Anger!

A nger is like an angry bull
N ever smash objects
G rowling like a dog
E vil is the devil
R aging like a sun burning.

Kai Hart (10)
Throston Primary School, Hartlepool

Happy

H appiness is flowing inside of you
A s the sadness is leaving, you are no longer blue
P ositive feelings flying around
P eople yelling, being loud
Y ou are happy, stay that way, watch that sadness stroll away.

Benjy Millward (10)
Throston Primary School, Hartlepool

Happy!

My colour when I think of happy is yellow.
The animal I think of when I am happy is a rat.
I think it smells like lavender swishing in a field.
It sounds like a tiny mouse squeaking for its mother.
When I feel a rat it feels like the fluffiest bunny in the world.

Millie Brown (7)
Throston Primary School, Hartlepool

Anger

A nger, you are a monster, you just come out without warning
N aughty is like Anger, they work together
G rating my teeth is the attitude it likes the best
R eally Anger, you're not the best
Y ou Anger, you erupt like a volcano, you know you got me in trouble.

Erin Elizabeth Frankland (10)
Throston Primary School, Hartlepool

Joy

Joy is pink like candyfloss
It smells like nature's trees
It looks like the beach has free boats
It sounds like a horse galloping
It feels like the only chance to laugh.

Ryan Kelsey (8)
Throston Primary School, Hartlepool

When Anger Strikes

A nger hides deep down low
N asty complaints makes anger come out
G ood friends turn on me and all they do is laugh at me
E veryone is mean to me so why not be mean back?
R age bubbles inside me!

Stanley Ridgway (9)
Throston Primary School, Hartlepool

Anger

A ngry feelings inside of me.
N asty comments said about me.
G reen makes me mad because I am always sad.
E lephants drive me crazy because they're always eating daisies.
R ed lollipops make me angry because they're always grainy.

Caleb Christal (9)
Throston Primary School, Hartlepool

Joyful

Purple as a present for a space party
It tastes like cake - great!
It feels like yummy chocolate
It sounds like you won't jump for joy.

Alisha Osborne (8)
Throston Primary School, Hartlepool

Happiness

Happiness is as cool as a rainbow in the sky
It can hear the crowd in the streets
It is playing football on the green grass
You can smell the sweet shop too!

Ben Goodwin (9)
Throston Primary School, Hartlepool

Anger

Anger is red like the Devil
It is flaming but it tastes like blood
Anger is fire from a bonfire but sometimes we have to be mad
Anger is red like the Devil.

Louis Weatherill-Smith (8)
Throston Primary School, Hartlepool

Excited

Excited is a yellow yolk
It tastes like yellow yoghurt - yuck!
Excited is a yolk food like a yellow teddy
It smells like warm yucky yoghurt.

Jessica Swinburne
Throston Primary School, Hartlepool

My Anger!

When I get angry I see a pool of red
My anger is like the living dead
If I push you over, your tooth will be hanging, cut by a thread
I'm extremely angry when I'm in my shed.

Ryan Picknett (10)
Throston Primary School, Hartlepool

Joyful

J oy is all around, so just be jolly!
O ut and about with my dolly.
Y ay, you're full of glee and delight.

Kate Muir (10)
Throston Primary School, Hartlepool

Happy

The colour of happy is light blue and bright yellow.
The smell is like lovely chocolate sweets.
The feel is like a lovely fluffy bear.

Sam Littlewood (7)
Throston Primary School, Hartlepool

Spiders, Spiders Everywhere!

Scary spiders give me a fright.
I just might run in fright.
Run in the bathroom, hide in the closet,
Get the fly splatter, run and get help!
Giant hairy spiders climbing everywhere
And clattering down the stairs.

Walking step by step,
Laughing and running down the hall,
Whimpering and wailing as they fall off the wall,
Hiding under the couch and one is trying to take a bath,
All the spiders are having a laugh and running about.

Some of them are in the kitchen, standing on the food,
Most of them are on the wall, in the living room,
They are bouncing on the bed, then one is in my room,
They are in the living room, watching cartoons.
I am standing in fear, why are they here?
When my dad comes with a shoe
All the spiders scurry out the room
Running for safety because he has a shoe!

Jasmine Leigh Pallent (9)
Whale Hill Primary School, Middlesbrough

Love

I bubble inside you and fill you with joy
And you stare at him which you enjoy.
I warm your heart again once more,
You find looking away a giant chore.

I wear a beautiful red dress,
When you look at me you are relieved of straining stress.
When you look at me you fear no more,
Like I am a puppy who you adore.

I live in your heart like a rooster in a nest,
It might be small but you get lots of rest.
I am protected by two lungs and a cage,
When you're annoyed just turn the page.

If you want to keep me give me a smile,
I will smile back and I will stay for a while.
I also come out when you're gobsmacked
And remember I do not lie.
Who am I?

Owen Harrison (10)
Whale Hill Primary School, Middlesbrough

Excitement In Disneyland

Waiting excitedly at the entrance to Disneyland,
Skipping happily towards the rides for me,
Standing in the queue with joy and giggling with glee,
As I drag Mum and Dad by the hand,
Running with hair-raising speed,
Looking for food.

My eyes are shining, smiles gleaming,
Screaming with laughter,
My happiness is a beam of sparkling sunlight on a summer's day,
Leaving the best till after,
And wanting to stay.

Lillie-Mae Kelly (10)
Whale Hill Primary School, Middlesbrough

Rumble, Rumble, Rumble!

As my tea is placed in the oven,
Two hours on my clock.
My belly is rumbling like an earthquake,
My belly about to *pop*.
Waiting, hands flat on the oven,
My mouth's watering like a turn on/turn off tap.
As my mum opens the oven,
My fingers start to tremble.
One hour left,
Rumble, rumble, rumble!
Shouting down the stairs, I hear my mum,
'Don't eat until the guests are here!'
As the guests arrive a flood of happiness
Comes over me.
Eating very fast, immediately it's all gone.
A yawn, a rub of an eye,
My hunger is gone, time for beddy-byes.

Faith Savage (10)
Whale Hill Primary School, Middlesbrough

Make A Best Friend

Joy is always there to be your friend,
Because her kindness will never end.
She lives in your head with lollipops and love
And her favourite animals are the doves above.

She's like a flower that never dies
And she'll never tell a lie.
Her hair is bright blue
And when she's really happy she boils up like stew!

You will never let her leave
And if she does leave you'll grieve.
So always be happy and she will never ever leave.

Grace Robinson (10)
Whale Hill Primary School, Middlesbrough

Feeling Blue

I feel like the sea, deep and blue,
Alone in my own cloudy world without you.
Salty tears have a race down my face,
And I sit silently in the corner of empty space.
Waiting for the clouds of denial to clear,
And my dreams of emptiness to disappear.
My mind is spinning
But my sadness is winning.

Waiting for the sun to shine through,
Someone can help but I don't know who.
Like a giant crushing hopes,
We needed to overcome many slopes.
Together we should have done life,
You took a gamble and rolled the dice.
I am overwhelmed with dread,
That I won't see you again.

Katie Marie Power (10)
Whale Hill Primary School, Middlesbrough

Happiness In Winter

It's Christmas Eve, I'm playing in the snow,
Having fun with my little bro.
The snow is all white and soft,
Getting the tree out of the loft.

Ripping open presents with joy and fun,
Running and jumping, I shout hooray!
But no more blazing sun,
Playing games, at the buffet.

It's Boxing Day already over,
Oh look, I found a clover.
Finally, the sun is back,
I'm going to play with my friends in a pack.

Elle Stainthorpe (10)
Whale Hill Primary School, Middlesbrough

Beach Excitement

Going out for the day,
I put on my new clothes,
Butterflies in my stomach,
After my nightly daze.
A day at the park?
A day at the beach?
How about one of each?
At the beach the waves crash like a stampeding rhino,
Splashing about in the salty sea,
The sun is a shining torch,
In a tranquil, turquoise blanket.
The long grass dances in the breeze.
I gaze around in wonder,
Excitement bubbles up inside me,
As I begin to ponder,
What will we do tomorrow?

Alix Huskison (10)
Whale Hill Primary School, Middlesbrough

The Angry Day

Clenching fists,
Punching the innocent doors,
Trashing my bedroom,
Screaming at everyone in my way,
I'm just having an angry day!

Stamping my feet,
Like a stampeding rhino,
Throwing things around,
Don't care if anyone's in my way,
Thinking of excuses to say,
I see my mam every day,
I just feel like saying, 'Go away!'
But I don't say.

Lilymae Hayes (10)
Whale Hill Primary School, Middlesbrough

The Miserable Football Match

Stomping around my room,
Like a depressed zombie searching for brains,
I lost that match against the school of doom,
That could have been my best game
I ever played, sprinting, tackling, getting the ball,
Happiness was in the air,
But now I'm just having a ball,
That team never plays fair!

Now I'm crying buckets of sadness,
I'm a cloud on a sunny day,
My manager says I'm the very best,
Trampling through the rest,
I'm louder than a foghorn,
Cheekier than the rest,
I'm never playing football again!

Halle Cole (10)
Whale Hill Primary School, Middlesbrough

The Creation Of Love

Our first talks,
Going to the pub,
Meeting in the mall,
Kissing in the club.

He's my diamond,
Getting engaged to my true love,
Hour after hour I get more flowers,
Moving together into our dream home.

We make a great bond,
We're now Mr and Mrs,
Sitting round the pond,
Sharing our kisses,
This is the rhythm of life!

Ellie Halliday (10)
Whale Hill Primary School, Middlesbrough

Home From Hospital

I was all alone,
And not at home,
The doctor said, 'You can get out of bed.'
Everyone shouted, 'Yes!'

When I got to my heart-warming house,
I felt like a miniature mouse.
I walked in and scrambled to my room,
My mum said, 'Warning, it looks like a torture tomb.'

I climbed up the swaying stairs with a heart full of joy,
I thought I'd see a big old toy,
Instead I saw a log,
Which was actually a dog!

I cried with surprise and joy,
He had a big bundle of toys.

Hannah Portas (9)
Whale Hill Primary School, Middlesbrough

The Angry Boy

Clenching fists angrily,
Punching walls,
Stomping upstairs like a stampeding rhino,
Pulling other people's hair nastily,
Banging doors loudly,
He is like a terrifying bull charging at a red flag.

Shouting horribly to people that makes people upset,
He blames other people so he doesn't get told off,
He goes up in his tidy room and breaks all of his toys and things,
His anger erupts like an overflowing volcano,
Screaming at people all day,
I am just having a bad day!
I see my dad and my mam every day,
I just feel like saying, 'Go away!'

Abbie Gibson (10)
Whale Hill Primary School, Middlesbrough

Happiness

Happiness is a dream
Happiness is a big disease
It is the best disease you've ever seen
And it makes you fill with ease
Happiness is a good emotion
And it makes you help people
Happiness is my thing
Happiness makes you want to sing
Happiness is the bestest emotion
It makes you want to help homeless people
It makes you give people things for free
And if you do they'll soon flee
But then you ought to ask why do you have to leave?
Even if you ask them I doubt that they'd come back
Because they'll want to spread the news.

Jack John Roberts (10)
Whale Hill Primary School, Middlesbrough

Excitement

The excitement of Christmas is always a joy,
Watching the girls and boys play with their toys,
The snow is white and extremely soft,
Getting the Christmas tree out the loft.

Ripping open presents is always fun,
It's now winter, no more sun,
The snow's falling very fast,
We're having a race, I'm sadly last.

At last dinner is finally done,
Everyone's had amazing fun,
Now everyone has gone home,
I'm suddenly feeling all alone.

Riley Graeme Kast (10)
Whale Hill Primary School, Middlesbrough

Anger!

When you feel Rage
He comes along and shoulders Joy.
He's not kind, trust me, oh boy!
When he takes over you don't act your age.
Everyone is scared of him,
I wonder why!
He makes everyone say, 'Goodbye,'
And he makes everyone feel grim.
When you burn your arm there's an alarm
And Anger springs to life,
Filling your life with dread and hate.
Trust me, he's a deadly fate.
You don't want to get on his bad side,
His only side.
What emotion is he?

Jack Edwards (9)
Whale Hill Primary School, Middlesbrough

The Poem Of Desperation

My house is a disgrace.
It is empty.
It is no longer a happy place . . .
We used to have plenty.

My property has been taken.
What should I do?
Please tell me who did this?
Was it you?

Please help me.
I have nothing left.
Help me please.
I feel bereft!

Evie Hopper (10)
Whale Hill Primary School, Middlesbrough

Anger Feelings

You are a rocket of rage
Knocking away everything in your path
Insulting people of every age
Everyone fears your wrath
When will you break out of that imaginary cage.

At school everyone stares at you like you're green
But in reality it's that you're mean
You glare at them
They all look away
You scream in rage and pull someone's hair.

That was a very unwise dare
Now you're expelled from the school
Yeah, now who's so cool?
Now you might realise you got too angry.

Harley Cruickshank (10)
Whale Hill Primary School, Middlesbrough

Joy, A Best Friend

Joy is a cuddly bear,
She will always be there for you,
When your mood needs a lift,
She will be happy to help you.

She lives on the brightest star in Candyland
And helps the bees,
She loves sweet treats,
She never gives up hope.

Because she's a flower
And rides her pet mouse, Cheese,
Who's nothing like his owner
'Cause he's a groaner.

Eleasha Nicole Love (9)
Whale Hill Primary School, Middlesbrough

Anger, The Worst Nightmare

Anger is the colour red
Anger is a cloud above your head
Anger makes you kick and scream
Anger is a thing that is always mean

Anger is a threatening cloud
Anger is a thing that can't be hidden
Anger is a thing that bothers you day and night
Anger is a thing that hurts your head

Anger feels like a hit in a face
Anger is a hand that won't let go
Anger is a hand that grips on tight
Anger smells like a smelly old sock.

Ryan Biggs (9)
Whale Hill Primary School, Middlesbrough

Worry

Worry is really deep
Worry is too black
Worry makes me leap
Worry makes me slam my door

Worry makes me pry
Worry makes me sad
Worry makes me cry
Worry makes me mad

Worry drives me crazy
Worry makes me scared
Worry makes me lie on my bed
Watching the people stare.

Jacob Stockton (9)
Whale Hill Primary School, Middlesbrough

Joy

Joy lives in my soul.
She never grows old.
She smiles all the time.
It feels like she's trying to climb.

She is a beautiful queen.
She is so not mean.
She likes her tiara shining,
That's why she is never whining.

I keep her happy
By not being snappy.
She is like a shining star,
Who is never too far.

Milly Reed (10)
Whale Hill Primary School, Middlesbrough

Make A Best Friend

She lives in your heart which is as red as a rose.
She will never disappear.
She will lift your emotions.
You can always count on her.
She has yellow skin and blue hair.
She also has a green dress with a yellow pattern.
To keep her all you need to do is turn on the light
So open the friendship door
And she will come in.

Who is she?
A: Joy.

Macie Hellon (9)
Whale Hill Primary School, Middlesbrough

Love

As we hold hands I feel love,
My love for him is as big as life,
I lay awake dreaming about our first kiss,
My love is a beam of light,
Hugging, kissing under the moonlit sky,
Love is way up high
Where the stars twinkle in the night,
We go out together to the mall,
At the prom we danced under the glitter ball,
We die holding hands,
Forever love will be in our hearts.

Cerys James (10)
Whale Hill Primary School, Middlesbrough

Sadness

Sadness lurking inside everyone's heart
Sadness grabs you with its fierce hands
Sadness is a pounding heart bouncing

Sadness sounds like a sad song
Sadness is a terrifying monster
Sadness is a hard, grey lightning storm

Sadness makes you cry
Sadness makes you feel sick
Sadness looks like the colour blue in light
Sadness makes you feel dull all day and all night.

Jessica Adamson (9)
Whale Hill Primary School, Middlesbrough

All About Love

Love is like a romance and flirty flowers.
Love is like a pink and red colour.
Love looks like a flower, she has a red dress.
Love is hearts and pink hair flowing down her neck.
Love sounds like a flirty love heart.
Love always talks about love with her fluffy voice.
Love feels like a bag full of love.
Love has never been seen.
Love smells like flowers in a bag.
Love is in each little flower with much colour.

Helena Dixon (9)
Whale Hill Primary School, Middlesbrough

Silliness Is So Cool

Silliness comes to play when you're joking around,
He's funny and joyful,
He's nice to be around.

Silliness comes to play every day,
He loves playing pranks
And thinking of jokes to say.

Silliness is a jester,
Silliness says silly stuff,
Silliness is like a joking master.

Owen Harding (10)
Whale Hill Primary School, Middlesbrough

Happiness

H appiness is here
A s the sunshine is bright
P resents come from family
P eople come to play
I n the bright light
N ight is coming
E mbarrassing my family for gifts
S taying for tea
S at watching television after a long day for me.

Lewis Clark (9)
Whale Hill Primary School, Middlesbrough

Happiness

Happiness is light purple and bright yellow.
Happiness feels like the warm summer sun.
It tastes like mint chocolate chip ice cream.
It makes me feel loved inside and out.
I feel happy when it's Christmas
Because I get to spend time with my family and I get presents.
Happiness makes me feel safe and warm.
I smell the sea water when I am happy.
I can hear children laughing when I am happy.

Sofia Bentley (9)
Whale Hill Primary School, Middlesbrough

Happiness

H appiness is yummy yellow with a bright blue shirt
A lways hugs her all day and all night
P eer all around, no sadness, no crying, only joy, that is all
P eer again, someone is sad, what should we do?
I will call Happiness, you wait here
N earby is Happiness, the girl runs to get him
E ssential gifts are given to the boy that is sad
S ad he is not for all he wanted was a gift
S ad is no more in this world, for evermore it will always be happy!

Sean Mullarkey (9)
Whale Hill Primary School, Middlesbrough

Anger Is Naughty

Anger screams loudly in my throat.
It smells like a house burning to the ground.
Anger looks like a demon.
It hugs me tightly whilst holding onto my lungs.

Anger sprints like a vicious bull coming towards you.
It burns like a fire in my heart.
Anger will never go away from your body.
It will if you try to do something happy or exciting.

Preston Hayes (9)
Whale Hill Primary School, Middlesbrough

Anger

Anger is a dark black shadow.
Anger makes me want to break free.
Anger is like a wolf howling.
Anger smells like dusty battered books.
Anger is a huge red monster
With a suit and tie on so he looks like he's the boss.
Anger is going to get you,
So you better watch out!

Sophie-Leigh Wanless (10)
Whale Hill Primary School, Middlesbrough

The Day I Fell In Love

I met a boy in the mall,
After that we had our first call,
We kept talking, the days were magical,
One night we went to the pub,
Then something beautiful happened,
I said yes.
We are soon to be married.
What is yet to come?

Leyla Rukiye Duran (10)
Whale Hill Primary School, Middlesbrough

Sadness

S orrow swirls down my spine.
A fraid to cry and run.
D evastation envelops me.
N ever to run away and cry.
E very day my heart falls to pieces.
S orrow streams down your back.
S adness makes you feel like you're going to be sick.

Adam Lincoln (9)
Whale Hill Primary School, Middlesbrough

Joy Riddle

This one is easy to explain
She never stops smiling
She's the opposite of sadness
And makes everything good
She's got blue hair
And shines like the sun.
What emotion is she?

Madalyn Ruby Horton (9)
Whale Hill Primary School, Middlesbrough

Happiness

Happiness is bright pink.
It tastes like chocolate muffins.
Happiness smells like fresh honey from a hive.
It looks like a magical garden.
Happiness sounds like children laughing with joy.
It makes me smile.

Alisha Massey (9)
Whale Hill Primary School, Middlesbrough

Happiness

Happiness is as white as snow.
It looks like you're flying free.
It sounds like joy is passing by.
It feels like white snow is passing by you.
It's like light colours are like wild winds easing by you.
The smell is like slow water dripping down your spine.

Danielle McKittrick (9)
Whale Hill Primary School, Middlesbrough

All About Anger

Anger is like a great ball of fire.
Anger is like a red and orange colour.
Anger sounds like a furious heart beating fast.
Anger feels like a crossed heart pounding.
Anger smells like fire being blown out.
Anger acts like an earthquake landed.

Jasmine Colpitts (10)
Whale Hill Primary School, Middlesbrough

Anger

A nger is a death machine
N aughty Anger will punch and fight to the death
G rowling Anger is a thunder and lightning storm
E veryone has anger in their thumping heart
R ubbish Anger is lurking inside you. It is a vast feeling.

Larry Parsons (9)
Whale Hill Primary School, Middlesbrough

Young Writers Information

We hope you have enjoyed reading this book – and that you will continue to in the coming years.

If you're a young writer who enjoys reading and creative writing, or the parent of an enthusiastic poet or story writer, do visit our website www.youngwriters.co.uk. Here you will find free competitions, workshops and games, as well as recommended reads, a poetry glossary and our blog.

If you would like to order further copies of this book, or any of our other titles, then please give us a call or visit **www.youngwriters.co.uk.**

Young Writers
Remus House
Coltsfoot Drive
Peterborough
PE2 9BF
(01733) 890066 / 898110
info@youngwriters.co.uk